Old Cheam

A photographic record and commentary

Compiled by
FRANK BURGESS

Design. Shirley Edwards.
Published by Sutton Libraries and Arts Services.

Introduction and Acknowledgements

THIS booklet has been inspired by the many people who have asked, nay, even urged me to write a history of Cheam on the strength of the mass of local information which I have acquired whilst assembling my now unique collection of old photographs of the village and surrounding area. These requests have come from members of audiences who have seen my slide shows illustrating Cheam, past and present, and I really believe that their enjoyment stems more from the pictures themselves than from my accompanying patter, although the two are of course complementary. It is for this reason that I have adopted the form that this volume takes rather than a more formal 'history'. The result is very similar to *All Our Yesterdays,* which was a pictorial record of the whole of the London Borough of Sutton, from the Libraries' collection, published in 1977.

In the span of history the period of the camera is but a moment, about 100 years, the span of memory of the present older generation and their parents, so it is the era that we can most fully understand and enjoy. One of the reasons that we continue to refer to Cheam Village, although it is now in the Greater London conurbation, is that it was still a small country village fifty years ago, which means that there are still many persons living who spent their early years in the village and who still refer to it as such.

I came to the district in 1938 when the development was at its height, and as a local government engineer here for 35 years I personally have been involved in many of the changes that have taken place. In 1971, as I approached retirement, I became interested in making copies of old photographs of the district. This was quite unpremeditated and no-one, least of all myself, foresaw where it was going to lead. Interest grew, and from an initial selection of 40 pictures from the Sutton Central Library archives (which were very soon afterwards to be supplemented by a considerable acquisition from the winding-up of the post-card publishers, Friths of Reigate), I was able to put together a show, *"Past & Present".* Since that first showing in 1971 I have given over 250 shows, and, after each one, members of the audience have offered old pictures to me for copying, with the result that I have now 700-800 negatives covering the old Borough of Sutton and Cheam.

It is of course impossible to name all these generous-hearted members of the public, but this foreword gives me the opportunity to acknowledge gratefully my indebtedness to them all, as a publication such as this could not have been compiled without their help.

To these good people who have helped me so much, the pictures will undoubtedly bring back youthful memories whilst my accompanying notes will only be trivia compared to those lifetime memories; but to the new residents and the younger generation I hope they will be of great interest and will give them an insight into the village life of the past.

There are less than 100 photographs reproduced here, which has meant quite a selection problem. This I approached on the basis of first, rarity; secondly interest; and thirdly, but not least, reproduction quality. With these three aims in view it has meant that some of the subjects which the reader might expect to find included are, if not wholly omitted, dealt with in a briefer manner than they deserve. The notable example is Whitehall, but this property is of such interest that it warrants a booklet to itself.

In the comments accompanying each picture I have tried to stick to facts and eschew hearsay and 'old wives' tales', but of course in quoting from earlier records of local history one can easily fall into the trap and innocently pass on hearsay. In the conviction that I will somewhere herein have done so, I ask the reader's indulgence. Regarding the date of the prints, in a number of cases this is actually known, in which case the date alone is given, but where a judgement has had to be made, C. for circa precedes the date. Finally, as redevelopment nowadays is so frequent and rapid, reference to 'today' can only be taken to mean 1978, and not at the time of subsequent reading or reprint.

I cannot leave unmentioned the debt we all owe to the old photographers themselves. Although the names of one or two of these are known, the great majority are lost in obscurity, but I nevertheless acknowledge my indebtedness to them all, known or unknown. Without their skill in the early days of photography we would not know what our village looked like 100 years ago.

Mention must also be made of my two written sources of information, namely *C.J. Marshall's History of Cheam & Sutton:* and *J. Morgan's & W.R. Church's Almanacs* for the years 1862 to 1880. All are valuable founts of knowledge of the history of the district, and their names appear frequently wherever I use information from their writings.

In addition to the general acknowledgement made earlier to the owners of photographs, I also wish to apologise to anyone whose susceptibilities might be affected by the use of a particular picture or pictures in this publication without specific permission.

I am also sincerely indebted to Mr Roy P Smith, FLA, Borough Librarian, for his acceptance of this volume as a companion to *All Our Yesterdays,* and for undertaking the publishing. My grateful thanks are also extended to members of his staff who have so willingly given of their time and expertise, without foreknowledge of which I would never have undertaken the project.

F.B.
Milhall, Cheam
1978

ISBN 0 9503224 5 8
Available from: Sutton Libraries & Arts Services, St. Nicholas Way, Sutton, Surrey. Tel. 01-661 5050
Printed in Cheam by J.W.Dunn (Printers) Limited

Station Road (now The Broadway) 1890

In this rural village scene the finger-post points to Ewell and Epsom to the left, and to the Railway Station behind the photographer. Although the railway came to Cheam in 1847 it did not precipitate the development of the area, which remained substantially unchanged for a further sixty years. Morgan observed in his account for the year 1878 under 'Cheam', "If new buildings and new streets are the best signs of progress, then Cheam is most certainly not moving with the times . . . the only new dwelling-houses built in the village this year have hidden themselves in a pit!" and the following year he was to say, "the hand of the builder still leaves this pretty village almost untouched."

Cheam's First Station C1900

In 1847 when the Epsom and Croydon line of the London, Brighton and South Coast Railway came to Cheam, the population of the whole parish was little over 1000 persons. Allowing that at least half of them would live in or around the village, it still does not amount to many potential travellers, particularly when most of the rural residents would use the train only rarely.

It might be thought that a greater justification was the proximity of Cheam School, whose pupils came from all over the British Isles, but here again the figures belie the thought, as in the 1840s there were only 60 pupils, nearly all of whom were boarders needing the use of transport only at vacations.

There is not, of course, any photographic evidence of what the locality was like before the railway was constructed, but hints can be gleaned from old maps. A sandy lane led south from the village up onto the Downs, which had to be bridged over near the junction of what are now known as Sandy Lane and Burdon Lane. From this point northwards through the village as far as Park Road it became known as Station Road. Marshall refers to alterations to Cheam Court on the corner of Ewell Road and

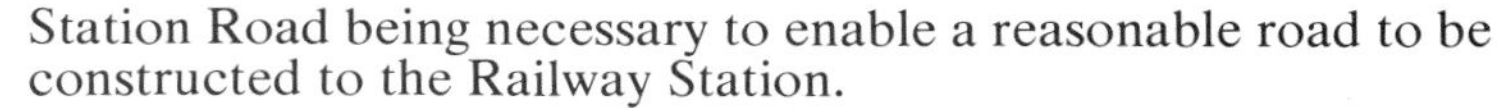

Station Road being necessary to enable a reasonable road to be constructed to the Railway Station.

There were two more tracks to the south, which had to be accommodated, recognised today as Manor Road and York Road. The former then existed as a lane alongside Manor House School (the one-time name for Cheam School) leading to the Church Farm land to the south. This was a large farm and its land extended as far as Belmont, and the brick-arch bridge shown in the picture was necessary to preserve access from the farm near the church, to the fields. For many years the tenant farmer was a Mr. Hales, and the large concrete by-pass road bridge is known as Hales Bridge even to this day.

What is known today as York Road was then also only an access track from the Sutton-Cheam road to the agricultural land, and the railway company made the necessary provision by means of a narrow low bridge of the type known as a 'cattle-creep', under which modern traffic still creeps in single file!

The Old Signal Box C1900

The New Station C1920

These two views show the widened four-track station in the days of steam, the layout of which has puzzled many people over the years. At the turn of the century the railway company became concerned at the loss of suburban passenger traffic to the newly-introduced electric tramways, and they sought ways to meet the challenge. One conclusion reached was that maybe the answer lay in electrification of the suburban railway routes. This was tried, and the electrification of the line out to West Croydon proved so successful, with overhead conductors, that the decision was taken to extend it as far as Cheam. This required the provision of marshalling and turnround facilities whilst still maintaining through-tracks for main-line steam trains. As some of these main-line trains would stop at Cheam, four platforms would be required, and four tracks required the widening of the three bridges, so all this work was put in hand. Before it was completed, however, the policy had been changed. Electrification was proving so successful that the railway company decided not only to standardise on the third-line conductor system, but not to stop at suburban lines, and electrify the whole main-line network. This, of course, made the terminal facilities at Cheam quite unnecessary and the centre island platforms were never built!

However, electrification proceeded, and the new trains commenced running through Cheam in 1929. With the provision of extensive goods-sidings on the south side of the line in 1909 the new station did an about-face and the main entrance and booking hall were built off the new road recently opened-up called Upper Mulgrave Road. Ticket facilities were, however, maintained on the up platform until about 1965. It can be seen that the small brick-arch bridge was replaced by a long multi-span bridge over the new tracks and sidings. This was only a narrow-track steel bridge to carry the farm traffic along Manor Lane, and in 1927, when the by-pass road had to be accommodated on this alignment, this narrow bridge became obsolete. Being less than 20 years old it was still a 'new' structure, and the railway company were able to find a good use for it. At that time a long foot-bridge was required to cross the tracks at Guildford station, where it was re-erected and remains in use to this day.

An Express going through C1920

Malden Road (now The Broadway) C1920

The redevelopment of the village which commenced in 1921 took place roughly in four stages, in the four quarters subdivided by the two main roads. The first section was the north-west segment on which stood the brewery; Cheam House; the old cottages in Park Lane belonging to the estate; and one or two other small premises, notably the Old Cottage and a baker's and general store.

The brewery was demolished in 1921, followed soon after by Cheam House, and the redevelopment of this land made possible the widening of portions of both Ewell Road and Malden Road. The fact that these two frontages were the first to be set back had the effect of reducing the stagger of the cross-roads, although not completely eliminating it.

The picture above shows the Old Cottage on the left-hand side, beyond which are the trees of Cheam House estate. The cottages on the right remained until 1932.

The Old Cottage awaiting Demolition 1921 

Although both the new frontages were ripe for shop development, it is a little surprising that one of the first new buildings in Ewell Road was a residence, a chalet bungalow occupied for many years by a veterinary surgeon and only demolished and replaced by shops (nos. 22a & b) in 1970.

The widening of Ewell Road from Park Lane to the cross-roads was completed without interruption, but it was not so in the case of Malden Road. Three buildings remained in the way, the Old Cottage, the baker's shop, and the general store. The Old Cottage, acquired in 1921 by the Highway Authority, was considered of sufficient merit to justify its preservation, so it was dismantled and moved to a new site, further back and a little way along the road, where it stands today in use as a shop.

The Old Cottage is thought to have dated from about 1500, but in the dismantling, signs were found suggesting that a lot of the timbers had been used prior to their use in the cottage, and this gave rise to a suggestion that maybe it was constructed from one of the buildings pulled down when Henry VIII razed the nearby village of Cuddington to clear the land for the building of Nonsuch Palace.

It would originally have been an exposed timber-framed building, infilled with wattle and daub panels, but, as was quite usual, when these deteriorated, lapped boarding was added to keep the structure weatherproof. This can be seen in the view taken before removal, and some early pictures also indicate that the floor was below ground level which must have resulted in considerable dampness. When reconstructed, this was remedied by raising the whole structure, which can be seen by the higher level of the ground-floor window-cills. Over the years numerous alterations had been made, but, in the rebuilding, the architects endeavoured to reconstruct it as originally built. The two most noticeable points are the relocation of the door from the front to its earlier position on the side, and the omission of the weather-boarding. To make the latter unnecessary in the future, the infilling of the panels was carried out in concrete. After the rebuilding was completed in 1922, the cottage was used as Cheam Parish Council's Office until 1928, when it was used as the Parks Superintendent's Office until more accommodation was required in 1953.

Thereafter it remained empty (with the exception of a few old artifacts) with public access on request, until it was leased as a shop in 1966.

Throughout the whole period from 1922 to 1962 it is an interesting fact that it was cleaned weekly by the same lady! — a remarkable record of continuous service.

 Shortly after Reconstruction 1922

The Old Cottage C1920

This view shows the situation before redevelopment commenced, with the cottage in its original position; and that on page seven, taken from approximately the same position, shows the progress made in four years.

In 1920 the cottage was in use as a cycle repair shop, and a sign of the trade, i.e. a cycle wheel, can be seen mounted on the gable of the building. Also can be seen the low level of the window-cill previously referred to, indicating a semi-sunken ground floor.

The high brick wall encloses the corner of the Cheam House estate, and in the background can be seen the brewery buildings.

The staggered cross-roads afford a good view of the Plough public house, and, in the distance, down Station Way, the house now converted and used as an optician's.

The Partially Redeveloped Village 1924

This 1924 view shows the Malden Road as it approached the cross-roads, with the newly-built shops on both sides, and the cottage on its new site. The vacant plot alongside carries a notice announcing that it is the 'Site for Sainsbury's Cheam Branch', which opened in 1931 and traded there until 1971.

Although the carriageway is not fully widened, the alignment with Station Way appears to be much improved; but unfortunately the next quarter of the village to be re-developed, i.e. the south-west, resulted in the west side of Station Way being set back, thus recreating the stagger, albeit not as great as originally. Across the cross-roads can still be seen the Plough public house, but the widened road now reveals Cheam Court farmhouse on the right-hand corner.

Malden Road, shortly to be renamed The Broadway C1926

The baker's shop referred to earlier was not acquired until 1932, by which time the west side of the road had been substantially developed, but the widening of the carriageway was not carried out, as can be seen from this photograph.

The single-storey bakery, and the shop beyond, projected for two-thirds of the width of the new road. Although the new shops on the west side enjoyed a wide footway, the street was not yet a 'Broadway', and it is interesting to see the large trees of the old estate still growing in the footway. Sainsbury's three-storey building is not yet built, enabling a view of the high gable of the building on the corner of Parkside to be seen. This gable carries an intriguing coat of arms in stonework; the ownership and origin of which have so far eluded all efforts to identify them.

Malden Road, passing between The Parochial Rooms and The Baker's Shop C1920

Looking South from Parkside 1922

These two views along Malden Road, as it was then called, again show the unwidened carriageway in an age when cars could be driven down the centre of the road with some degree of impunity. There is nevertheless a record that the Council at the time were preoccupied with the problem of car-parking on the wide gravel verge on the opposite side to the parochial rooms!

Whilst this early development was taking place, Cheam was still a parish within the Epsom Rural District. It wasn't until 1928 that the Surrey Review Order allocated Cheam to the Urban District of Sutton and the whole then became Sutton and Cheam Urban District. It was at this time that a great many 'double-barrelled' authorities came into being as parishes were amalgamated. Beddington and Wallington; Merton and Morden; Malden and Coombe; Epsom and Ewell; Walton and Weybridge, were a few examples. It seems a pity that they had such a short life, and, since 1965, many of them have lost their identity within the new larger authorities whose boundaries and new names will take years to become household knowledge.

As is so often the case in a developing area, the provision of shops lagged behind the residential development, traders being reluctant to establish businesses until demand can be seen to exist. This is shown to be the case in Cheam by a perusal of the statistics of population and new streets, etc.

Year	*Population*	*New Streets*
1901	3404	—
1911	6200	—
1921	7843	38
1926	—	56
1931	18510	106

The number of residential roads trebled in the ten years in which the shop development commenced; little wonder that the green fields disappeared! An almost similar increase can be found in the railway traffic, and, as with the traders, it followed the demand: 39 trains to town per day in 1881; 97 per day in 1936.

Looking South from the Bakery 1922

Mrs. Rowe's Sweet Shop and Old Cottages, The Broadway C1933

At last, twelve years after the commencement of the redevelopment, the baker's and the general stores have gone, but the wide pavement remains, the country's financial crisis of the early 1930s having deferred the widening of the carriageway. The cut-back single-storey bakehouse can be seen, and, in the absence of the general stores, the cottages which stood behind it are revealed, and have become the new frontage. These cottages line up nicely with Whitehall and the other cottages to the north, and, as they are considerably older than the shop was, it is difficult to understand how the shop ever came to be built in front of them. It is easier in the case of Mrs. Rowe's shop, as it appears to be simply a single-storey structure built on a front garden. Even this projected too far and was eventually cut back to enable the widening of the carriageway to be completed.

The general widening of this portion of Malden Road was carried out in the middle 1930s, having been renamed The Broadway in 1930.

The Cross-Roads C1920

This view over the cross-roads, looking along Malden Road, shows again the considerable staggered alignment that then existed and which is still evident in the present-day roads. The prominent building on the corner of Ewell Road is part of the old-established Cheam Brewery. There is pictorial evidence that at one time the corner of this building was square, thus causing a greater stagger to the cross-roads, but that at sometime after 1840 it was rounded-off as shown here, to improve the corner.

It is interesting to note that, in nearly all the old photographs of the junction, the village policeman is present, and that in 1920 even an infirm pedestrian could stand in the carriageway in comparative safety.

Cheam School C1835

At the top of High Street was Cheam School, often referred to as Tabor's School, and even as Manor House School on early Ordnance sheets. It stood where Tabor Court stands today between the by-pass road and Dallas Road. It was built in 1719 and remained there until 1934. It has the reputation of being one of the oldest-established private preparatory schools in the kingdom, and many of its pupils became very eminent personalities, one of the last such to attend the school at Cheam was, indeed, His Royal Highness Prince Philip, Duke of Edinburgh.

This engraving from a drawing by T. Maisey, art master at the school, shows faintly on the right-hand edge the stable for the head-master's horse. This small building survived until the late 1950s as the builder's office on the corner of Dallas Road.

Cheam House from Malden Rd. C1910

Cheam House, already referred to, occupied most of the land embraced by Park Lane, Ewell Road and Malden Road, and stood on a north-south alignment across what is now Parkside. (A distinction must be appreciated between this house and Cheam *Park* House, which was a quite different estate within Cheam Park itself.)

It was built about 1770 by John Pybus and the original entrance is said to have been in Park Lane, as, in those days, the Malden Road was but a cart-track. Over the years it was occupied by some eminent persons, but in 1914 it was empty and was used to accommodate German prisoners-of-war. At the end of hostilities the whole estate was purchased for development and the house was demolished in 1922.

As can be seen, the grounds were quite extensive and well laid out. Many of the larger trees are still to be seen growing in the back gardens of the houses in Parkside. It was when the new houses were being built that a mediaeval pottery kiln was unearthed and a great many shards were found along with quite a number of whole pots of various shapes and sizes. These were of such archaeological interest that the kiln itself was removed and set up at the Science Museum in South Kensington, and over a hundred of the pots were distributed between the British Museum, the Victoria and Albert and the Guildford Museum. Others were retained and for many years were on display in The Old Cottage, before going into store for some years. Cheam Pottery can now be seen again in Cheam Village; but this time in Whitehall, recently opened to the public.

Cheam House from the garden C1910

Cheam House Grounds C1900

Cheam Square C1890

Both these photographs show properties which stood on the east side of Malden Road but both are now obliterated by the modern development. Cheam Square is referred to by Mr Marshall, who tells us that it was located behind the early Plough public house which stood on the north corner of High Street at the cross-roads. The photograph, which, from the character of the original might well be over 100 years old, shows the rear of the building that was previously the Plough, and the children are presumably standing in Cheam 'Square'. It seems strange that a small village should sport a 'square'; but Carshalton also had one, and indeed the name still exists there, although the square, as such, has long gone.

Necton stood in The Broadway, alongside the drive leading to the Doctor's surgery, until 1965, when it was demolished to make way for a 'supermarket'. It started life as a single-storeyed building on the land used as the kitchen-garden across the lane from Cheam House, but, during the development of the village, a second storey was added and the whole adapted as a residence of character.

Necton C1930

Old Wrought-Iron Gates 1923

It was on the frontage of the kitchen-garden that, Mr Marshall tells us, stood a pair of wrought-iron gates, which, it is said, came originally from Nonsuch Palace or West Cheam Manor. During the redevelopment they were removed and offered for sale. In the right-hand picture a photograph has been taken to show the detail of one of the gates and its frame. The location of this photograph was in the blacksmith's yard at the smithy below the signal-box beside the Station Way railway bridge.

At least one of the pair was purchased by a gentleman who was building a house at Thames Ditton, and the photograph below shows the gate in its new position today. Is it too much to hope that one day it may find its way back home to Cheam?

The Cheam Gate at Thames Ditton C1975

Station Way C1910

In 1910 Station Way comprised little more than the property shown in this view. The entrance to Cheam Court Farm was just off the picture to the left; nearer to the railway station was the Railway Inn, with some cottages in the pits on either side of the approach to the railway bridge.

In those days there was only this one shop in the road, built on half of the original front garden of a house. Today all the gardens in the row are wholly occupied by shop extensions and the original is the only one with an open forecourt.

The Railway Inn and Station Way Pit

These views are particularly interesting as they show the old wooden cottages which used to be in the pit behind the Railway Inn. Originally there were nine cottages and a smithy, but the latter moved up onto the highway by the railway bridge in 1860. It is often thought that this pit, which can be seen on the site to extend behind the houses on the east side of the road as well as the main pit on the west, was excavated to build the railway embankment. This is not likely to be so, as the railway was only constructed in 1846 and according to Marshall a smithy had existed in 'the old quarry' for many years.

Although the smithy left the pit in 1860, the cottages remained for a further 76 years, being vacated in 1936. The land has not been filled and developed because it receives the surface water from a considerable distance down Sandy and Burdon Lanes and acts as a gigantic soakaway. To find an alternative outlet for this water would prove immensely expensive.

◀ **Station Way Pit C1910**

Station Way Smithy and Bridge C1900

In 1900 the bridge over Station Road consisted of the brick arch only; the steel girder bridge which can be seen there today was built alongside in 1907 when the tracks were duplicated, as explained earlier.

On the left is the smithy, established there in 1860, and over the bridge can be seen Coldblow on the corner of Peaches Close, where Mr Boniface the brewer lived.

The Century Cinema 1950

One does not need to have lived in Cheam for more than twenty years for this picture to bring back pleasant memories of epic films of earlier years re-shown at the Century Cinema, yet it is surprising how many present residents are quite surprised to learn that the office block behind the present petrol station started life as a cinema. It was built in 1937 and closed in 1960, when the entrance foyer was demolished and the petrol filling station constructed.

Cheam Court Farmhouse C1925

Part of this old farmhouse, which stood on the corner of Ewell Road and Station Road, was built as a 'hall house' in early Tudor times and was considerably added-to in later periods. It was not as substantial as it appears; it consisted of brick, chalk and flint only up to first floor level. Above this it was a timber-framed building clad with laths and stucco.

Marshall says that some of the original house was cut away in 1845 to enable Station Road to be built to give adequate access to the railway station which was then being constructed.

Cheam Court Dairy

Cheam Court Farm, Cheam.

~

Only HOME PRODUCED MILK sold by my carts.

The Cows are inspected by the Local Authorities at regular periods.

Samples of the Milk are analysed frequently so as to keep up the standard of Purity and Quality.

N.B. The Cows can be seen any afternoon after 2.30, excepting when there is any epidemic of illness about, either human or cattle, when no one excepting the milkers are allowed in the sheds.

P. C. KERR.

Both these illustrations constituted an advertisement card; the picture on the face and the type matter on the back. The establishment was quite a large dairy farm with a large barn, which can just be seen in the previous picture, and twelve other barns and cow houses. In 1929 the business was purchased by United Dairies, who transferred it to new premises built on one of the meadows further down Ewell Road, where it is still operating today. The old farm was then put up for sale and the buildings were bought by the Saint Dunstan's Parochial Church Council, to provide materials, in the form of oak timbers, to use in the construction of a daughter church which was urgently needed in the Gander Green Lane area of the parish to meet the needs of the rapidly developing district.

The project came to fruition in 1933, in the form of Saint Alban's Church on the corner of Elmbrook Road and Gander Green Lane; often referred to as the Barn Church.

Old Saint Dunstan's 1860

This engraving of Saint Dunstan's, published in 1860, shows the old church with its external stairs to the galleries. This building, with the exception of the chancel, was demolished in 1865, after the new church had been put into use. This sequence was possible as the new church was built alongside the old one; not, as was the usual custom, on the same site. Although the new church was opened in 1864 it was not actually completed, with the construction of the spire, until 1870.

Old Saint Dunstan's C1850

In this view the most prominent portion of the old church is the south-side chapel which was demolished with the nave and tower. The chancel, on the right, can be recognised as the present Lumley Chapel. This portion of the old church contained the major monuments to the Lumley family, and it was retained to house all the other tablets and memorials to the Lumleys, from other locations in the church, before it was destroyed. This Chapel and its interesting contents is most beautifully preserved and is open to members of the public upon request at the address displayed on the door.

Cheam Park House C1930

Cheam Park House, here illustrated, stood on the north side of the present park with its back to the walled nursery garden. This location was nearer the centre of the original park, which stretched northwards as far as where Hemmingford Road is now.

This park, and the house, were bought by the Local Authority in 1937, when Mrs Bethel, the resident owner, died. One of the last purposes to which the house was put was for the assembling of gas-masks in 1939-40. It came to the end of its life in 1944 when a flying-bomb landed in the park and damaged the house beyond repair.

Cheam Volunteer Fire Brigade 1912

Before the days of the Boroughs' or Counties' fire services, each parish had its own voluntary brigade, with a manual pump and light ladders. In Cheam, the small Fire Station to house the equipment was on Pond Hill between the Rectory and the Institute, the latter now the 1st Cheam Scouts' Headquarters. This photograph, taken in front of the Fire Station, was of the brigade in 1912 when they won a challenge shield in a brigade competition.

The small notice on the station door reads:

Keys with Mr Bastin,
at the 'Prince of Wales' opposite

Mr Bastin, second from the left, was chief of the four-man brigade as well as being the publican of the Prince of Wales!

At the outbreak of war, even the up-to-date Borough Fire Brigade had to be supplemented to meet the threat of incendiary air-raids; the A.F.S. (Auxiliary Fire Service) was recruited, and equipped with trailer pumps which could be drawn by private cars in the early days.

Another use made of the recently-acquired Cheam Park buildings was the housing of the initial delivery of these pumps in the old coach-house and stables in the park; until special accommodation could be made at strategic points.

The squad pictured here, photographed in Anne Boleyn's Walk, were housed in a war-time building on the adjacent cinema car-park.

A Cheam A.F.S. Squad 1940

Whitehall C1910

Whitehall, built in about 1500, is one of the few remaining 'gems' of the old village. It has attracted artists and photographers for the past 150 years at least, and a great number of photographs have survived. As mentioned in the foreword, the premises justify a publication to themselves, but this photograph is included here to depict the rural atmosphere of the village in the early years of the century. The house is now in the care of Sutton Libraries and Arts Services and open for viewing.

The Red Lion C1875

Another photograph of 'the old days' when there was time 'to stand and stare'. According to Marshall, this building would now be nearly 400 years old. It is still the main structure of the present 'pub', although various additions over the years have given it a very different appearance. On the extreme right of the picture can be seen the well-head which is still preserved on the forecourt today.

Park Lane C1910

In 1910 the cottages in Park Lane belonged to the Cheam House estate. Shepherd's premises were 'dog-legged' in plan, consisting of the shop in Park Lane and a cart-shed on Malden Road, with the bakery in between.

This bakehouse and cart-shed is the one referred to earlier which projected into the new wide road eventually named The Broadway.

These cottages standing next to the Red Lion were probably as old as the inn. They were certainly very poor sub-standard dwellings in the late 1960s, when they were pulled down and replaced with modern 'town houses'.

The old well-head outside the Red Lion can be seen on the left, and on the right is Bay Cottage, said to have been built of materials from Nonsuch Palace.

At one time Park Road was known as Red Lion Street, and the portion from Malden Road, past the Red Lion into Church Farm Lane, (alongside the wall of West Cheam Manor) was the Market Furlong referred to by Charles Marshall, where the annual one-day Cheam Fair has been held on May 15th since 1259.

Cottages in Park Road C1930

Old Cottages, Malden Road C1900

Little is known of these cottages other than that they stood in Malden Road on Pond Hill, immediately below Sergeant's Pond Hill Dairy, just about where Tudor Close joins Malden Road, and were demolished about the turn of the century.

The original of this picture is in Sutton's Local Collection, and until recently was unidentified although it was recorded as being somewhere in Malden Road. It is now confidently believed to be the artist's impression of the same cottages on this page, painted from the opposite direction.

It is an interesting example of the difference often found between a photograph and an artist's impression. Not only has the artist made a 'picture' of a few very run-down cottages, but they are depicted on a comparatively level road, whereas Pond Hill, Malden Road, is a considerable incline.

Water Colour of Malden Rd Cottages

Mr. Corbett's Cab C1925

The location of this group photograph is the forecourt of Mr. Corbett's premises in Ewell Road, where, until 1975, Nonsuch Motors garage and filling-station stood. On the left was the coach-house and stable, and behind the cab can be seen the residential accommodation. Mr. Corbett plied for hire at Sutton Station and his was the last horse cab to do so into the middle 1930s.

The Queen Victoria Inn C1910

This Public House, which stood right on the corner of Malden Road and London Road, remained, albeit in a modernised state, until 1936, when a very large modern 'house' replaced it behind an extensive forecourt, and the road junction was laid out for the increasing traffic. In 1964 the new 'Vic' was demolished and a smaller version incorporated in the extensive commercial redevelopment of the site.

Quarry Hill, Cheam Road   C1910

Seventy years ago, the area between Cheam and Sutton was very undeveloped, consisting of large estates or fields, but nevertheless with plenty of trees. This is shown in this view of the main road looking towards Sutton from where the by-pass road now crosses.

Not a house in sight, the only sign of habitation is the cap of a gate pillar and the sign 'Carriage Drive' at the entrance to The Quarry, a house that stood where the Quarry Park Road estate is now.

Love Lane C1920

An alternative way to Sutton, avoiding the 'traffic' of the old turnpike road, was along the footpath known as Love Lane, from Saint Dunstan's Church to Saint Nicholas' Church at Sutton. This started from Church Road between the Lych Gate and the high wall of West Cheam Manor, round which it went to the corner of Park Road at the Red Lion. From this point it struck east in an almost direct line to Sutton.

The picture on the right is where a path joined from the south on what is now the track of the by-pass road. The wooden gates are the rear gates of The Quarry House and are in this position to this day.

The lower picture shows the footpath winding its way eastwards past 'Boney Hole' as it was called. This is the low spot where in wet seasons the ground-water used to rise to the surface and flow away northwards as a bourne. This happened severely in 1925-26 and it was in the very near vicinity that the water company put down their Cheam wells in Gander Green Lane.

A little way beyond this point the path crossed Gander Green Lane and made its way to Sutton on the line of Tate Road, Western Road and Camden Road.

Chalk is a good water storage medium, like a sponge; but so much water is extracted these days that it does not rise to the surface as a bourne in Cheam any more, and is very intermittent at Ewell and Carshalton. The water which appears nowadays in the pond in Cheam Park, and the pit in Station Way, is not bourne water but surface-water run-off from the public highways.

Our piped water, however, still originates from the chalk uplands via the deep wells of the Sutton District Water Company, which, like the old settlements, are located where the chalk dives below the London clay.

No illustration has come to light showing a communal village pump or well, but the locations of many wells are known from the old Ordnance sheets. It appears that most of the substantial establishments had their own private well, but groups of cottages shared one. A well-head and winch is still preserved outside the Red Lion in Park Road, and a photograph exists of the Whitehall well. Until a few years ago the Water Company used regularly to dip remaining wells to record the ground-water level and the one in Cheam Park nursery-yard was on their list.

Bourne Hole C1910

Tollhouse and Gates on Cheam Turnpike Road 1881

The toll roads constructed through Sutton in 1755 had a toll house and gates at the cross-roads at the Cock Hotel, but in 1837 they were moved further out to embrace the development of the town which at that time could already be foreseen.

The Cheam Road gate was moved to the junction of Gander Green Lane, and the toll house was built on the south-west corner of what is now York Road.

The above artist's impression is dated 1881, one year before the tolls were abolished, and depicts a lady and her dog proceeding towards Cheam.

Cheam Hall Farm C1900

This is a view of the rear of the farmhouse which stood on the 'S' bend in Gander Green Lane.

The origin of the name Gander Green is obscure, but the fact that it was a country 'lane' is well confirmed in the many old photographs which have survived.

The children here are sitting on the verge of the lane just about opposite where Bourne Way is today.

The buildings on the right of the picture are on the other side of the 'S' bend and are in the Lower Cheam House estate in the grounds of The Lodge, where Antrobus Close was built about 1950.

Gander Green Lane fifty years ago

These are two views which depict the character of the 'lane'. The pond (above) was on the north side, half-way between the 'S' bend and Sutton West Station, and remained there until the turn of the century.

Gander Green Lane is a long road, but one clue in the picture on the left remains today to enable us to identify the exact spot. The building on the right-hand edge is the front of the most north-westerly pair of the row of five pairs of cottages backing on to Hamilton Avenue. This puts the group of buildings on the left at the end of Kingston Avenue, on Brock's Estate; it is in fact Brock's Fireworks factory, which dates the picture to about 1920.

Brock's Fireworks C1925

Brock's Crystal Palace Fireworks were world-renowned. The firm's reputation was already well-established when it moved to Cheam in 1901, where Crystal Palace Fireworks were made and exported to all quarters of the globe for the next 30 years.

During the 19th century, accidents during firework manufacture caused great concern and it was not until the beginning of the present century that dispersal of risk was accepted as one of the best insurances against large tragic accidents. Brock's new works at Cheam was based on this principal, spread over the whole of the land now occupied by the large housing estate within the Gander Green Lane, Windsor Avenue, Marlow Drive perimeter.

The explosive materials and processes were all handled in small quantities in small sheds and bunkers dispersed all over the site, connected to the central unit by light narrow-gauge railway.

A great number of the work-force were women and girls; and those who handled the 'black powder' in the filling sheds wore black boiler-suits, (above) and the 'Bon-Bon' makers and packers and dispatchers wore white overalls. (left)

At their peak of popularity, pyrotechnic displays surpassed any seen since the war. In 1919 Brock's received an order for the most extensive display ever, and this was put on in Hyde Park. Some idea of the magnitude of the event can be got from such statistics as:— "Shells of calibre 16″ down to 5½″ in salvoes of fifty at each discharge, 1 lb rockets in flights of a hundred at a time with a final flight of 2000. Roman candles in batteries of 200 and a cascade of fire 1000 feet in length"—all made in Cheam!

Cheam Hare Warren C1925

South of the village stood a hare warren traditionally thought to be connected with Nonsuch Palace. At the time it was built, it was in open country, but is now embraced by Warren Avenue, Wilbury Avenue and Onslow Avenue, the fourth side being behind the properties at the bottom of Scarborough Close.

This was, in effect, a wild copse of about 11 acres, surrounded by a high brick wall, incorporated in which was a keeper's lodge at the north-east corner, through which was the only access to the warren.

The age of the warren is not known, but it is shown on some very early maps and some of the brickwork is thought to be Tudor. Amongst the multitudinous graffiti is to be found 'E.W. 1753' in a very convincing style of lettering and figures of the period.

The use to which it appears to have been put was the breeding of hares within the confines of the warren to provide sport in coursing by letting them out through purpose-made escape-holes in the wall.

These holes were normally closed with shutters, and it is an interesting fact that holes are only located in the Onslow Avenue wall facing *due west,* which would have the result that the 'chase' would have the sun behind them instead of in their eyes.

The warren is now almost wholly occupied with residences, but fortunately large sections of the wall remain, showing the flint foundation and the nicely built escape-holes.

The Warren Lodge C1930

Two recent photographs showing the warren wall today

Wall in Onslow Avenue

Detail of Escape Hole

Warren Farm C1920

The location of this farm should not be confused with the hare warren; they were over a mile apart. The farm was situated between the Croydon to Epsom Railway and Nonsuch Park, immediately to the north of the arch beneath the tracks at the bottom of Bramley Road. The lane shown in the picture now forms the footpath through the present-day agricultural land to Nonsuch Park.

Harvesting in Cheam fifty years ago

The precise location of the haymaking (above) cannot be ascertained, but it is a nice reminder that this was an annual event in Cheam well within living memory.

The note on the back of this old photograph (left) simply said 'between Burdon Lane and Sandy Lane' but the exact location has been ascertained after close scrutiny of the horizon on the original print and found to be south of the hare warren between High View and Downs Side.

Now The Broadway C1910

Let us take a last look at a view which shows Cheam as it was before the redevelopment began. By this date the brewery had closed down, and the notice at the gate on the corner of the Old Cottage suggests that Baker's Motor and Cycle Works were established in the old brewery yard, to meet the needs not only of cyclists, but also of motorists.

In the days of water-bound macadam roads, the name meant what it said — 'water-bound', and they became unstable if allowed to dry out completely, in addition to which they became very dusty. To prevent this the roads were regularly watered during the summer from a watering-cart with sprinklers on the back. The one shown here is being filled from a fire-hydrant which can still be found in the same position outside No. 4 The Broadway, and today is used also for watering the adjacent flower-beds.

Nick's Grave, Cheam House Garden C1900

It might be thought appropriate to end this look at so many things of old Cheam that have disappeared, with an epitaph. This wooden tablet stood in the grounds of Cheam House at the graveside of Mrs Pybus' pet dog Nick. The epitaph below, which it carried, is believed to have been composed by Sydney Smith, author and wit, who married Kitty Pybus, daughter of Nick's mistress.

Here lies poor Nick an honest creature.
Of faithful, gentle, courteous nature.
A parlour pet, unspoiled by favour,
A pattern of good dog behaviour.
Without a wish, without a dream
Beyond his home and friends at Cheam.
Contentedly through life he trotted
Along the path that life allotted:
Till time his aged body wearying
Bereaved him of his sight and hearing,
Then laid him down without a pain
To sleep and never wake again.
Reader, do'st thy reflection tell
Thou livest so wisely or so well?
If not, go mind thee wilst thou mayst,
And take example from a beast.
For many a gentleman may pick
A lesson from the life of NICK.

Aerial view, 1932, looking due north. Amongst the many items of interest to be seen, the following are a few worth noting. Scanning across from left to right one can pick out:-

Houses in the Priory Road and Abbots Road area, Matlock Crescent laid out without any buildings, and the new by-pass road curving away towards the Gander Inn.

The chimney of the disused Cheam brickworks, below which is Tilehurst Road and Kingsdown Road being developed, and Fromondes Road almost complete. Alberta Avenue and Perrot's brickworks over the by-pass road.

Tudor Close, the first half of Lumley Road, Saint Dunstan's Church, Lumley Gardens 'U'-shaped carriageway without houses, and Spring Close Cottages, Seears Park, and Quarry Cottage over the other side of the by-pass.

Park Road with the Baptist Church on one corner and White Lodge opposite, Stafford House and its paddock upon which Stafford Close was built.

The developing Broadway with Sainsbury's new building completed, but still with the general stores restriction. White House where Farnham Court now stands.

Ewell Road north side shops complete, including Chamberlain's veterinary surgery. Norrington's on the corner of High Street, demolished, (site not built on until the 1950s).

United Dairy Depot, Cheam Motors, and Cheam Court flats with shops below, with open land to the south on which the cinema was built in 1937. Across the road, allotments where Cheam Mansions were built.

Open land on either side of Anne Boleyn's Walk and Kingsway Road. The Railway Inn and the Station Master's house opposite.

New houses in Anne Boleyn's Walk, cottages in the pit behind the Railway Inn, and the cottages in Station Way as it runs down to the railway bridge.